RACHEL WOJO

Confident Trust

believing God's plan is best

BIBLE READING PLAN
& JOURNAL

CONFIDENT TRUST
Bible Reading Plan and Journal
PUBLISHED BY RACHEL WOJO
Copyright © 2017 by Rachel Wojnarowski

Visit **www.rachelwojo.com/shop**

Requests for information should be addressed to rachel@rachelwojo.com

Trade Paperback

ISBN-13: 978-0692866375 (Rachel Wojo LLC)

ISBN-10: 069286637X

Cover design by Rachel Wojnarowski

Photo credit: Bigstock.com

Library of Congress Cataloging-in-Publication Data

Printed in the United States of America
2017—First Edition--1001

Table of Contents

Table of Contents

A Personal Note from Rachel

Dear Friend,

Thank you for joining in to experience a newfound trust for God and his word. My goal through Bible reading is to draw closer to Jesus, and I want that for you too!

Through reading daily Bible passages, praying, and listening to God, we're going to nurture and grow our relationship with him. This Bible reading plan and journal is specifically focused on confident trust in God's plan and promises.

Whether experiencing tough times or enduring everyday situations, it's easy to turn to our own solutions and forget that God is worthy of our trust. He has never changed and never will. This Bible reading plan serves as the reminder that his love for us insists on his perfect plan for our lives.

O for grace to trust him more!

I.can't.wait!

Rachel

Believing God's Plan is Best

Welcome to the Confident Trust Journal. I'm so excited to begin this journey with you! For the next thirty-one days, we are going to dig into God's word and grow closer to Him. Together we'll make the choice to trust God and his word by reading and applying it in our daily lives.

> When things seem out of control, God is always in control.
> --*One More Step*

Are you ready to learn to trust God through every circumstance? You can share what you are learning on social media by using the hashtags #confidenttrustjournal and #biblereadingplan or you can just keep it between you and God.

4 Simple Steps

to growing in faith

step 1:

Pray: Spend some time with God in prayer. Prayer is simply having a conversation with him.

step 2:

Read the Bible passage for the day one time slowly, soaking in each phrase. Read again if time allows.

step 3:

Answer the daily question.

step 4:

Complete the journaling section.

Psalm 20:1-9

I have a choice to
place my trust in
the one true God.

What one thought
from the passage will
help me remember to
trust God?

_____
_____
_____
_____
_____
_____
_____
_____
_____

Today I will
Rest in God's promises,
Understanding He is
Sovereign and I can
Trust Him with:

_____
_____
_____
_____
_____
_____
_____

Refuge

God alone is my rock and salvation.

When I'm struggling to trust God, what fact from this passage would remind me He is worthy of my trust?

_____

_____

_____

_____

_____

_____

_____

_____

_____

Today I will
Rest in God's promises,
Understanding He is
Sovereign and I can
Trust Him with:

_____

_____

_____

_____

_____

_____

_____

_____

Isaiah 26:1-13

When I'm struggling
to trust God, what
fact from this passage
would remind me He
is worthy of my trust?

_____
_____
_____
_____
_____
_____
_____
_____

My God is great
and worthy of my
trust.

Today I will
Rest in God's promises,
Understanding He is
Sovereign and I can
Trust Him with:

_____
_____
_____
_____
_____
_____
_____

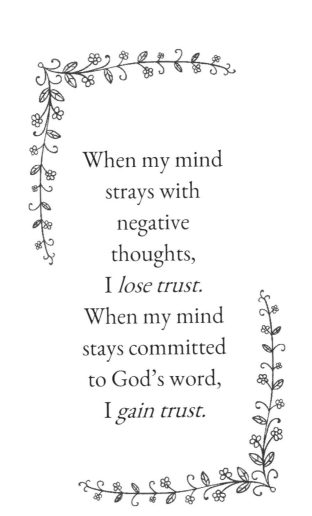

When my mind
strays with
negative
thoughts,
I *lose trust.*
When my mind
stays committed
to God's word,
I *gain trust.*

Commit

What one thought
from the passage will
help me remember to
trust God?

Worry is the
enemy of trust.

_____
_____
_____
_____
_____
_____
_____
_____

Today I will
Rest in God's promises,
Understanding He is
Sovereign and I can
Trust Him with:

_____
_____
_____
_____
_____
_____
_____
_____

What one thought
from the passage will
help me remember to
trust God?

God directs every
detail in my life.

_____
_____
_____
_____
_____
_____
_____
_____

Today I will
Rest in God's promises,
Understanding He is
Sovereign and I can
Trust Him with:

_____
_____
_____
_____
_____
_____

Delivered

When I'm struggling
to trust God, what
fact from this passage
would remind me He
is worthy of my trust?

My salvation is from
the Lord.

_____

_____

_____

_____

_____

_____

_____

Today I will
Rest in God's promises,
Understanding He is
Sovereign and I can
Trust Him with:

_____

_____

_____

_____

_____

_____

John 14:1-10

Promise

Jesus is the way,
the truth and the
life.

When I'm struggling
to trust God, what
fact from this passage
would remind me He
is worthy of my trust?

_____
_____
_____
_____
_____
_____
_____

Today I will
Rest in God's promises,
Understanding He is
Sovereign and I can
Trust Him with:

_____
_____
_____
_____
_____
_____
_____

Truth

The Holy Spirit
is with me.

When I'm struggling
to trust God, what
fact from this passage
would remind me He
is worthy of my trust?

_____
_____
_____
_____
_____
_____
_____
_____
_____

Today I will
Rest in God's promises,
Understanding He is
Sovereign and I can
Trust Him with:

_____
_____
_____
_____
_____
_____
_____
_____

John 14:22-31

Why Trust?

Because God is
love.

When I'm struggling
to trust God, what
fact from this passage
would remind me He
is worthy of my trust?

_____
_____
_____
_____
_____
_____
_____

Today I will
Rest in God's promises,
Understanding He is
Sovereign and I can
Trust Him with:

_____
_____
_____
_____
_____
_____

From the
beginning
of time,
the Creator
of the universe
has kept
His promise
to redeem
you.

Psalm 46:1-11

Present

God is my help in trouble.

When I'm struggling to trust God, what fact from this passage would remind me He is worthy of my trust?

_____

_____

_____

_____

_____

_____

_____

Today I will
Rest in God's promises,
Understanding He is
Sovereign and I can
Trust Him with:

_____

_____

_____

_____

_____

_____

Psalm 118:1-13

Triumph

The Lord is on
my side.

When I'm struggling
to trust God, what
fact from this passage
would remind me He
is worthy of my trust?

_____
_____
_____
_____
_____
_____
_____
_____
_____

Today I will
Rest in God's promises,
Understanding He is
Sovereign and I can
Trust Him with:

_____
_____
_____
_____
_____
_____
_____

Psalm 118:14-29

Day 12

Acknowledge

My God is known
to unleash His
power when I
praise Him.

When I'm struggling
to trust God, what
fact from this passage
would remind me He
is worthy of my trust?

_____
_____
_____
_____
_____
_____
_____
_____

Today I will
Rest in God's promises,
Understanding He is
Sovereign and I can
Trust Him with:

_____
_____
_____
_____
_____
_____

Proverbs 30:1-9

Truth

Every word of
God proves true.

What one thought
from the passage will
help me remember to
trust God?

_____
_____
_____
_____
_____
_____
_____

Today I will
Rest in God's promises,
Understanding He is
Sovereign and I can
Trust Him with:

_____
_____
_____
_____
_____
_____
_____

Trusting God is
a daily choice.

I can resist
and
gain nothing.
or
I can run to
Him
and
take refuge

Psalm 5:1-12

Believe

Knowing what
God loves and
appreciates gives
me the
opportunity to
trust Him more.

What one thought
from the passage will
help me remember to
trust God?

_____
_____
_____
_____
_____
_____
_____
_____
_____

Today I will
Rest in God's promises,
Understanding He is
Sovereign and I can
Trust Him with:

_____
_____
_____
_____
_____
_____
_____

Awesome

There is no god
like the Most
High God.

When I'm struggling
to trust God, what
fact from this passage
would remind me He
is worthy of my trust?

_____
_____
_____
_____
_____
_____
_____
_____

Today I will
Rest in God's promises,
Understanding He is
Sovereign and I can
Trust Him with:

_____
_____
_____
_____
_____
_____
_____

Psalm 86:10-17

Teachable

What one thought
from the passage will
help me remember to
trust God?

I must ask God to
teach me to trust
Him.

_____
_____
_____
_____
_____
_____
_____
_____

Today I will
Rest in God's promises,
Understanding He is
Sovereign and I can
Trust Him with:

_____
_____
_____
_____
_____
_____
_____

A willing servant
learns to trust God
quicker
than a worried saint.

Luke 12:24-31

What one thought
from the passage will
help me remember to
trust God?

Human reasoning
will not naturally
encourage a strong
trust in God.

_____
_____
_____
_____
_____
_____
_____
_____
_____

Today I will
Rest in God's promises,
Understanding He is
Sovereign and I can
Trust Him with:

_____
_____
_____
_____
_____
_____
_____
_____

Proverbs 3:1-8

Day 18

All In

I want to trust
God with
everything.

What one thought
from the passage will
help me remember to
trust God?

_____
_____
_____
_____
_____
_____
_____
_____
_____

Today I will
Rest in God's promises,
Understanding He is
Sovereign and I can
Trust Him with:

_____
_____
_____
_____
_____
_____
_____

Isaiah 50:4-11

Rely

I can rest and relax
when I choose to
trust God.

What one thought
from the passage will
help me remember to
trust God?

_____
_____
_____
_____
_____
_____
_____
_____

Today I will
Rest in God's promises,
Understanding He is
Sovereign and I can
Trust Him with:

_____
_____
_____
_____
_____
_____

Psalm 91:1-16

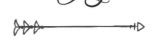

No Fear

Trust includes
answering God's
call.

What one thought
from the passage will
help me remember to
trust God?

_____
_____
_____
_____
_____
_____
_____
_____
_____

Today I will
Rest in God's promises,
Understanding He is
Sovereign and I can
Trust Him with:

_____
_____
_____
_____
_____
_____
_____

Jeremiah 17:5-10

Blessed

God promises
blessing when I
trust Him.

What one thought
from the passage will
help me remember to
trust God?

_____
_____
_____
_____
_____
_____
_____
_____

Today I will
Rest in God's promises,
Understanding He is
Sovereign and I can
Trust Him with:

_____
_____
_____
_____
_____
_____
_____

Blessed is the woman who
trusts in the Lord,
whose trust is the Lord.
She is like a tree planted by
water,
that sends out its roots by
the stream,
and does not fear when heat
comes,
for its leaves remain green,
and is not anxious in the year
of drought,
for it does not cease to bear
fruit.

Jeremiah 17:7&8

Psalm 78:1-11

Share

What one thought from the passage will help me remember to trust God?

Make His name glorious.

_____
_____
_____
_____
_____
_____
_____
_____
_____
_____

Today I will
Rest in God's promises,
Understanding He is
Sovereign and I can
Trust Him with:

_____
_____
_____
_____
_____
_____
_____

Psalm 78:12-29

Remember

God's promises
prove He is
trustworthy.

When I'm struggling
to trust God, what
fact from this passage
would remind me He
is worthy of my trust?

_____
_____
_____
_____
_____
_____
_____
_____

Today I will
Rest in God's promises,
Understanding He is
Sovereign and I can
Trust Him with:

_____
_____
_____
_____
_____
_____
_____

It is tempting to
long for answers on this earth.
It is enticing to
desire above-average knowledge.
It is prideful to
offer God solutions.
It is humbling to realize
God's plans are always bigger and
better than mine.
He is more than worthy of my trust.

Psalm 78:30-42

I should reflect on
the miracles God
has performed in
my life.

What one thought
from the passage will
help me remember to
trust God?

_____
_____
_____
_____
_____
_____
_____
_____

Today I will
Rest in God's promises,
Understanding He is
Sovereign and I can
Trust Him with:

_____
_____
_____
_____
_____
_____
_____

Psalm 78:43-55

Guidance

God leads people
out of wildernesses
every day.

When I'm struggling
to trust God, what
fact from this passage
would remind me He
is worthy of my trust?

_____
_____
_____
_____
_____
_____
_____
_____
_____

Today I will
Rest in God's promises,
Understanding He is
Sovereign and I can
Trust Him with:

_____
_____
_____
_____
_____
_____
_____

Under His wings
I am safely abiding;
Though the night deepens
and tempests are wild,
Still I can trust Him,
I know He will keep me;
He has redeemed me,
and I am His child.
Under His wings, under His wings,
Who from His love can sever?
Under His wings my soul shall abide,
Safely abide forever.

Hymn, Under His Wings, Authors Cushing &
Beck, Public Domain

Psalm 78:56-72

Day 26

Action

God promises to
shepherd and
guide my heart.

When I'm struggling
to trust God, what
fact from this passage
would remind me He
is worthy of my trust?

_____
_____
_____
_____
_____
_____
_____
_____

Today I will
Rest in God's promises,
Understanding He is
Sovereign and I can
Trust Him with:

_____
_____
_____
_____
_____
_____
_____

Psalm 115:1-9

Invisible

Tangible does not equal trustworthy; only God is worthy of our trust.

When I'm struggling to trust God, what fact from this passage would remind me He is worthy of my trust?

_____
_____
_____
_____
_____
_____
_____
_____
_____

Today I will
Rest in God's promises,
Understanding He is
Sovereign and I can
Trust Him with:

_____
_____
_____
_____
_____
_____
_____
_____

Psalm 115:10-18

Day 28

Respect

God is in control.

When I'm struggling to trust God, what fact from this passage would remind me He is worthy of my trust?

_____
_____
_____
_____
_____
_____
_____

Today I will
Rest in God's promises,
Understanding He is
Sovereign and I can
Trust Him with:

_____
_____
_____
_____
_____
_____
_____

Power

I want to rely on
the Holy Spirit to
guide me.

What one thought
from the passage will
help me remember to
trust God?

_____
_____
_____
_____
_____
_____
_____
_____
_____

Today I will
Rest in God's promises,
Understanding He is
Sovereign and I can
Trust Him with:

_____
_____
_____
_____
_____
_____
_____

Isaiah 43:1-12

Rest

I am his child and
He knows my
name.

What one thought
from the passage will
help me remember to
trust God?

_____
_____
_____
_____
_____
_____
_____

Today I will
Rest in God's promises,
Understanding He is
Sovereign and I can
Trust Him with:

_____
_____
_____
_____
_____
_____

The God who
calms
the storms
with His voice
longs to calm
the storms
of your heart
with His love.

The Lord delivers
protection over
every step.

When I'm struggling
to trust God, what
fact from this passage
would remind me He
is worthy of my trust?

_____

_____

_____

_____

_____

_____

_____

_____

Today I will
Rest in God's promises,
Understanding He is
Sovereign and I can
Trust Him with:

_____

_____

_____

_____

_____

_____

_____

Put a Bow on It!

You did it! You read your Bible for 31 days in a row!

Throughout this month of Scripture reading, I've been reminded our God is worthy of our trust and I'm so very grateful.

We trust God for eternal salvation; why not trust him for everyday solutions?

I pray that as you've walked this 31-day path, you've enjoyed learning to trust God more and you're feeling confident to rely on both his promises and his plan.

Thanks for joining me on this journey through the Bible. Discover more Bible reading plans & journals at rachelwojo.com/shop.

About the Author

Rachel "Wojo" Wojnarowski is wife to Matt and mom to seven wonderful kids. Her greatest passion is inspiring others to welcome Jesus into their lives and enjoy the abundant life he offers.

As a sought-after blogger and writer, she sees thousands of readers visit her blog daily. Rachel leads community ladies' Bible studies in central Ohio and serves as an event planner and speaker. In her "free time" she crochets, knits, and sews handmade clothing. Okay, not really. She enjoys running and she's a tech geek at heart.

Reader, writer, speaker, and dreamer, Rachel can be found on her website at **www.RachelWojo.com.**

Free Bible Study Video Series

If you enjoyed this Bible reading plan & journal, then you'll love Rachel's free video Bible study to help you find strength for difficult seasons of life! **http://rachelwojo.com/free-bible-study-video-series-for-one-more-step/**

Feel like giving up?

Are you ready to quit? Give up? But deep down, you want to figure out how to keep on keeping on?

Like you, Rachel has faced experiences that crushed her dreams of the perfect life: a failed marriage, a daughter's heartbreaking diagnosis, and more. In this book, she transparently shares her pain and empathizes with yours, then points you to the path of God's Word, where you'll find hope to carry you forward. One More Step gives you permission to ache freely—and helps you believe that life won't always be this hard. No matter the circumstances you face, through these pages you'll learn to...

- persevere through out-of-control circumstances and gain a more intimate relationship with Jesus
- run to God's Word when discouragement strikes
- replace feelings of despair with truths of Scripture

If you enjoyed this Bible reading plan and journal, then you'll love: